THE BATTERED PREACHER'S WIFE

Dr. Avril E. Wiggins

Copyright © 2007 by Dr. Avril E. Wiggins

The Battered Preacher's Wife
by Dr. Avril E. Wiggins

Printed in the United States of America

ISBN 978-1-60266-908-6

All rights reserved solely by the author. The author guarantees all contents are original and do not infringe upon the legal rights of any other person or work. No part of this book may be reproduced in any form without the permission of the author. The views expressed in this book are not necessarily those of the publisher.

Unless otherwise indicated, Bible quotations are taken from the Internet. Bible verses KJV: King James Version was taken from www.studylight.org. Amp: Amplified Bible taken from www.studylight.org. The Catholic Church responds to Domestic Violence and the poems were taken from www.usccb.org. The Black Church and Domestic Violence Statistics were taken from www.bcdvi.org. The dictionary references were taken from Merriam Webster Online www.m.w.org.

www.xulonpress.com

Table of Contents

Acknowledgement v
Dedication vii
Foreword .... ix-x
Introduction .... xii-xv
Chapter One 17
   The Beginning
Chapter Two 27
   The Example I Saw
Chapter Three 31
   Valentine's Banquet
Chapter Four 35
   He Said I was His Wife
Chapter Five
   The Wedding
Chapter Six 61
   The Final Blow
Chapter Seven 69
   My Friend's Story

Chapter Eight 73
Domestic Violence and The Black Church Statistics
Chapter Nine 77
The Catholic Church View
Chapter Ten 87
Conclusion
Chapter Eleven 91
General Information

Acknowledgment

Thank you God for being a father to me when my earthly one wasn't there when I needed him. You loved me when I didn't want to live and you are my daddy. I thank you for sending your only begotten son Jesus Christ to die on the cross for all of my sins, and my life is so much better because of your son. One day, I want to hear you say well done thy good and faithful servant. I love you with all of my heart.

Dedication

Dedicated to my family and all the survivors of domestic violence.

Bishop I.V. and Lady Bridget Hilliard (My Spiritual Parents.) I didn't have a choice concerning my birth parents, but I had a chose with my spiritual parents. Thank you for helping me to realize that all my dreams and visions are possible. You are the example of Excellence, Faithfulness, and hard work. You have taught me to endure hardness and never give up. Thank you for not being so busy to reach out to me when I really needed you. I love you so much.

Thank You, to Prophetess Juanita Bynum-Weeks for being an example of survival. You were someone that survived and let me know that I could survive as well. You may never meet me, but your life has helped me to press on with the things that God called me to do. I love and appreciate you.

Thank You, Mother Apostle Callie Jasper for letting me know that I could get out of that abusive marriage. You never stopped telling me that I didn't deserve to be treated like that and it was not God's will for my life. I love you so much.

To The Love of my life Eld. Joe Wiggins. You have always pushed me, supported me, and encouraged me to be all that God has called me to be. You are my gift from God.

To the Joys of my life Zipporah, Shekinah, Zithri, Josiah, and Micah. You all have sacrificed so much, and God is going to reward you all for everything. I love you so much.

Thank You, House of Rapha continue to hold on, God is going to make us great.

Foreword

By Calvin Moore, Jr., Ph.D.

The Phoenix Rises

In ancient Egyptian mythology and in myths derived from it, the phoenix is a mythical, sacred firebird. Said to live for five hundred or for one thousand, four hundred sixty-one years (depending on the source), the phoenix is a bird with beautiful gold and red plumage. At the end of its life cycle, the phoenix builds itself a nest of cinnamon twigs that it ignites. Both nest and bird burn fiercely and are reduced to ashes, from which a new, young phoenix arises. The new phoenix embalms the ashes of the old phoenix in an egg made of myrrh and deposits it in the Egyptian city of Heliopolis. The bird was also said to regenerate when hurt or wounded by a foe, thus being almost immortal and invincible: a symbol of fire and divinity. Although descriptions vary, the phoenix became popular in early Christian art, literature, and symbolism as a symbol of Christ, representing the resurrection, immortality, and the life after death of Jesus Christ.

In many ways, Dr. Avril E. Wiggins' life resembles the phoenix. Her life story reminds me of this great mythical bird that is said to heal itself after it has been hurt or injured by a predator. That is the great lesson of this text. No matter what life holds for us, we have the strength and fortitude to deal with it. The Holy Spirit helps us to deal with it, and like the phoenix we rise above all of our circumstances. Dr. Wiggins' testimony points to the power of the human spirit to survive enormous challenges. I have often wondered what was so unique about Dr. Wiggins that allowed her to conquer her fears and triumph despite overwhelming odds and debilitating situations that would have driven a lesser person to suicide. Then I remembered that she is saved, sanctified, and filled with the Holy Spirit. That is the assurance that all people need when facing difficult situations.

The myth of the phoenix is just that: a myth. However, the life of Dr. Wiggins is real, and so is her testimony of survival. When I fellowship with her, I feel as though I am in the presence of a phoenix. She would reject such a notion, choosing to instead point me to the "real" phoenix, Jesus Christ. Certainly He paid a price that none of us can take credit for in this life. Because of the work of Jesus on the cross, we are all able to rise like a phoenix. It is my hope that you enjoy this poignant and riveting story.

THE BATTERED PREACHER'S WIFE

Dr. Avril E. Wiggins

This book will discuss domestic violence in the pulpit. The information that will be discussed is true. Some of the research and other statements that are going to be used are taken from the Internet and will be noted when used. The individual's story will have altered names to protect the person's privacy. The term "batter" (taken from Merriam Webster's Online) means "to beat with successive blows so as to bruise, shatter, or demolish; to subject to strong, overwhelming or repeated attack."

Introduction

I was born in South Carolina to a teen mom who got pregnant at sixteen by a man five years her elder. The story told to me was that my mother was my dad's steady girlfriend. Prior to my conception, my mom thought she was pregnant and told my dad. It turned out she wasn't. Being a steady girlfriend doesn't mean you are in a committed marriage relationship. My dad was doing what a lot of young men do. He played the field. Not only did he get my mom pregnant, but he also got another young lady pregnant at the same time. I guess he was caught between a rock and a hard place. My dad was asked by the other young lady's mother to marry her, because she had a mean stepfather. In the meantime, while my dad was trying to make his decision about marrying this young lady, my mom found out that she was really pregnant, and of course, he didn't believe her. He thought she was just trying to stop him from choosing the other young lady. My dad made his decision, and he married the other lady. Then, as time went on, he saw that my mother was not lying. Her belly was growing with me inside. How I wished all my life he had chosen my mother and me. Don't get me wrong. I have a family of brothers and sisters that I love, but this is about me expressing my true feelings.

I longed for my father's love, and as I grew up, I felt abandoned by him. I didn't meet him until I was almost twelve, and the next time I saw him, I was seventeen. I always wondered why he didn't choose my mother. I always wanted my dad, needed my dad, and he wasn't there. I resented him and his whole family, because they had him and I didn't. My mother got married, but her husband abused her as well as my sister and me. We endured a lot of abuse, and I blamed my dad for letting it happen. I always felt that he should have done something to help me, but he didn't. He was just as much my dad as he was the dad to his wife's children. I shed a lot of tears, but God was always there for me. The dearest memory of my dad was the first time he kissed me on the cheek. I knew in that moment that he loved me, but in my eyes his love was not enough to save me from a childhood of abuse. His love for me never caused him to fight for me. I believe that if my dad were in my life, I would have made better choices in men. My dad has been married for over thirty-five years; he has six children with his wife. You have to respect the fact that he tried to be responsible for his actions.

I know my mother had to be devastated, but she moved on with her life. She ended up getting pregnant about two years after having me. That relationship didn't work out, and then about a year after that, she moved in with a man and had her third child. They eventually got married, but the relationship was trouble from the beginning. He started abusing her even before they got married. I have very vivid memories of him beating my mother for hours and abusing us as well. This went on for the majority of their marriage. They stayed married for twenty-five years. I never understood why my mother married him in the first place. He was already abusing her and abusing us. I guess she felt helpless being twenty with three children from three different men. Everyone called her a whore and called us bastard kids. You just get use to it. I never understood why my mom stayed for so long. She would leave, but she always came back. This is the example that I ended up following. My mother married him, even though he was abusing her before they got married. The average woman will end up marrying her abuser. This example set me on a destructive path. I say that because our parents are our first teachers. If my stepdad had embraced me as a daughter when I was growing up instead of another man's child, then I know our relationship would have been different. He didn't cover me as a father growing up, and it opened the doorway for further abuse from his family, who taunted me and always reminded me that he was not my dad. My stepdad is a Christian now, and I forgave him. We have a pretty decent relationship today, and I thank God for that. It was God's healing hand that healed all my wounds and helped me to forgive him and his family. You have to forgive in order to heal. I will reference forgiveness quite frequently, because that's what this book is about.

Chapter 1

The Beginning

Here's my story. I became a Christian at age eleven, which means that I accepted the Lord into my life and made Him my Lord and personal Savior. I make the distinction because a lot of times we ask Jesus to come into our lives, and we make Him Lord. We acknowledge Him as being the Son of God, but we don't make Him the Savior of our lives. We don't give Him control of our lives. We don't live our lives with Him being in the driver's seat. Romans 1:19-21 says, "For that which is known about God is evident to them and made plain in their inner consciousness, because God [Himself] has shown it to them. For ever since the creation of the world His invisible nature and attributes, that is and through the things made intelligible and clearly discernible in and through the things that have been made-His handiworks. So [men] are without excuse-altogether without any defense or justification. Because when they knew and recognized Him as God, they did not honor and glorify Him as God, or give Him thanks. But instead they became futile and godless in their thinking-with vain imaginings, foolish reasoning and stupid speculations-and their senseless minds were darkened" (AMP).

In 1985, I was a senior in high school preparing to graduate, when I met a very nice young man on the bus while coming from school. He just happened to be my neighbor. He was a very sweet and kind young man, but he wasn't a Christian. I knew that I shouldn't have gotten involved with him. I went against everything that I believed and was taught, but I did it anyway. I was looking for love, and I had a hole in my soul that I didn't allow God to fix. I wanted my daddy. I prayed a lot, asking God to heal me, but I never allowed God to do it. I needed a father's love, which I believe is so crucial for the development of girls into womanhood. The only positive male figures in my life growing up were my grandfather and my uncle. Although I was very close to them and they were always there for me, I still wanted and needed my daddy. I felt like I was robbed of him, and I just gravitated toward the first young man who showed an interest in me. I forgot about what the Word said, because the pain on the inside just wouldn't go away. I allowed this young man to pull me outside of my relationship with Christ. In other words, I fell into sin with him. I had a very committed walk with God all during middle school and high school, but when I graduated the enemy sent someone that was just the perfect gentleman. I became distracted from God and drawn to him. Let's look up the word distract (Merriam-Webster), which means "to turn aside, divert to draw or direct (as one's attention) to a different object or in a different directions at the same time. 2. To stir up or confuse with conflicting emotions or motives." That's what was happening to me. I was being pulled in a different direction, away from my relationship with God. The Bible says in 2 Corinthians 6:14, "Be ye not unequally yoked together with unbelievers. For what fellowship hath righteousness with unrighteousness, and what communion hath light with darkness?" We need to understand that we can't go against the Word of God (that is, if we are claming to be Christians) and expect God to bless our mess, wrong decisions, or unwise choices.

I disobeyed the Word of God, and I suffered. I turned my back on God for a man. In other words, I moved God out to move this young man in. I thought he showed me the love I was so dying for, but was it really love? Well, let's see what the Bible has to say concerning this. John 3:16 says, "For God so loved the world that he gave his only begotten son, that whosoever believeth in him should not perish, but have everlasting life." Our greatest example of love is God's example. He gave his only begotten Son. So love gives. Love is not how much I say I love you, it's how I show that I love you. Based on that, he didn't love me. He had a strong attraction; he was infatuated and full of what the Bible calls youthful lust. He really didn't care if he caused me to backslide. When someone loves and respects you, he will not put you in a position to cause you to sin. That's why the Word of God tells you, if you are a believer (Christian), not to get involved with someone who is not a believer. He just wanted what he wanted, and at that time, it wasn't God. Don't get me wrong. He had a lot of potential, but we were going in different directions. The enemy will and can send people into your life to get you distracted from God. John 10:10 says, "The thief comes not but for to steal, kill and to destroy and [Jesus said] I am come that they might have life, and that they might have it more abundantly."(KJV) I wasn't having abundant life being pulled away from God and being forced to make a decision that was against my Father God. Therefore, I gave the devil access to my life, because I disobeyed God's Word. I know this made the enemy happy. The devil could go to God and say, "Well! Look what I caused Your daughter to do. I caused her to be consumed with someone other than You." And he could say to God, "I got another one of Your committed ones to forsake You and turn her back on You for a man." That's exactly what I did. It's like idol worship. I lived this young man. He became my everything, and God is supposed to be your everything. I moved God out in my quest for love. One thing I want to make clear is that God must be first, and at that time, I became consumed by my desire for love. God says in His Word that "I am a jealous God and I will have no other gods before me." Exodus 20:5

Then the love of my life, the one that I turned away from God for, joined the military, and I was left alone with God. Without being distracted by the young man, everything in my life began to change. I began to see how I worshiped him. I was totally in love, and love became my god, my mission, and my purpose. I was totally committed to him, but he wasn't committed to me. He was young and immature. Isn't that how it goes, ladies? We become so consumed with the feeling that love brings, and we just forget about God when that man comes around. He could be ugly, snaggle-toothed, cross-eyed, or married, but none of that matters. And you know that just because the man or woman is separated makes them no less married; you need to run from that. Don't even get involved with that, because you end up hurting more people than yourself, including the wife or husband and their children. Whatever the case may be, it really doesn't matter. You just want to fill the hole in your soul; it feels like something eating at your gut, like a pain that just won't quit. I just wanted someone to help me heal. Even if it wasn't my daddy, as long as it was another man, I would take the substitute.

When love becomes your god, it causes you to become blind to the truth. You can't hear anyone else or see anyone else; you just become mesmerized by the attention that you are getting, the attention you never got from your father. It takes your mind off the pain, because it's like that person is starting to feed your pain. No one can tell you anything; you know that this is the one. We get spiritual amnesia and are like, "God who?" We just throw God away as if He wasn't enough. I would have to say that I became self-absorbed; everything was about my pain. Love became my god, my mission, and my purpose. Can you imagine how God feels? I had to face the fact that I hurt the One that has always loved me in my search for love. John 3:16 says, "For God so loved the world [and that's including me and you] that he gave his only begotten son, that whosoever believeth in Him should not perish, but have everlasting life." I know I made reference to this same Scripture verse earlier, but this Scripture verse is so powerful and life changing. You should just pause and think about that. Wow!

I gave up so much for this young man, and he had no respect for my relationship with God. When you settle for a relationship like that, someone is going to pull someone. The majority of the time, it is the unbeliever pulling the believer away from God, and that's what happened in my case. If you are the exception to the rule, then that is awesome. I do know of some cases where the lady or man didn't compromise and won the unbeliever to the Lord. It can happen, but in my case, because I had come from a dysfunctional family and was wounded, it didn't work out that way. Everything that I did, I did hoping he would love me, because I really didn't love myself, and I allowed him to pull me outside of my relationship with God. I told him I didn't want to have sex until I was married, and he refused to accept that. He said that if we loved each other, then it was okay. It's not okay. You see, he had no regard for what I believed. He kept trying until I gave in. I gave in for many reasons. Because I didn't have a good relationship with my stepdad and I didn't have a relationship with my biological father, I really wanted him to love me and not leave me. I thought that if I didn't he would leave me, and I gave in. I have always regretted that. If a man loves you, he will respect you and your desires. I found myself doing things with him that I should not have done. He was not my husband. I fell away from God, and the Holy Spirit left me. I felt like I was the walking dead. I knew that the fellowship and communion that I had once shared with God was gone, and that was the worst feeling in the world. I put being in love before God, and that hurt.

Like I said earlier, my boyfriend joined the military, and while he was gone he would write me. I felt like something wasn't right (you know we have that women's intuition). Well, the day came when I got a phone call from him. He told me that he had a fling with a young lady, that she was pregnant, and that it was a possibility that the baby could be his. I could not deal with that. I gave up my committed walk with God to please him. I thought that if I didn't give into him he would leave me or find someone else, and he did it anyway. He found someone else to do what he wanted, and he didn't consider me or my feelings. I felt betrayed, but again, he wasn't my husband. Ladies, we often fall into these traps, because we didn't have a father's love or validation in the home. I know this can happen even with a father's love and validation. But for me, I feel that if my daddy or stepdad would have just told me that I was beautiful or let me know that I was a good daughter or that they were proud to have me as a daughter, then I would not have felt like a fatherless child. I would not have been in search of love from a man.

The Battered Preacher's Wife

After the young man confessed to me what he had done, I just lay in my bed and cried like a baby. I felt like I was worthless and not worthy of love. I thought, *my daddy doesn't love me, my stepdad doesn't love me, and now this guy has broken my heart into a million pieces.* I had given him the greatest thing, myself, and turned my back on God for him, and he just trampled all over my heart. You have to be careful who you give your heart to. All I could do was look up to God. I hit rock bottom. I had become suicidal. I was committed to him, but he wasn't committed to me. I loved him, and I would not have done that to him. I gave up my greatest treasure, my body, in pursuit of love, and he found someone else to satisfy his flesh. I was crushed, devastated, and to make matters worse, he could have a baby with this girl. I felt like saying, "How could you do this to me? I turned my back on God for you." I couldn't believe this was happening to me. I became severely depressed, and my life began to take a downward spiral. I felt dirty, misused, and abused. What he did to me was just as bad as all the abuse that I had endured as a child. I began to feel that I wasn't good enough and to wonder how God could love someone like me after what I had done to Him. Thank God for His mercy and His grace; it never ends.

I ended up having a nervous breakdown. Let me go deep into why this happened to me. I was raped and sexually abused by a step uncle when I was around four or five. Both my sister and I were violated; she was two at the time. He put us in separate rooms daily, and he started touching, feeling, and doing all kinds of sexual acts which were beyond my understanding. I was only around four or five years old. After he had sex with my sister, he knew he had done some damage. He then gave her Clorox to drink to try to cover up what he had done. The Clorox damaged her insides, but she didn't die. And that's a miracle in itself. While in the hospital for drinking the Clorox that she was forced to drink, the doctor discovered that she was raped. The doctor told my mother that someone had raped my sister. My mother tried to talk to my stepdad, but she was unsuccessful at finding out what had happened to her. No one pursued it any further, and that was it. They didn't want to affect the young man's career; it didn't matter what he had done to us. My sister had surgery: they had to put her womb back in place. You see, after he raped me, I fainted. It was too traumatic; I was in and out of consciousness. I remember him taking me outside to the barn and doing his thing with me. I was thinking, *what is this thing*, and I went out. I had an out of body experience; it was like my spirit was looking at what he was doing to my body. I remember him picking me up, taking me inside, putting me in a tub of hot water, and washing me off. I just don't understand why we remain silent victims. I was saved but tormented inside by what had happened to me at that tender age. I had been to counseling and talked to people, but my mother didn't know that he had raped me until I was sixteen.

What my boyfriend did to me just opened that wound again. The only thing that helped me heal was the power of God, and I had to go back to prayer. I started back reading the Bible. I had to go back to my first love. It was God who healed me emotionally. I repented for what I had done, and God helped me get my life back together. I was thankful that the young man was honest with me. He was honest enough to tell me the truth about what he had done. What I have found out is that a lot of times we as women give ourselves, our bodies, over to men, and they don't have the same commitment level. I believe that's why a relationship should be based on getting to know one another, and sex should be reserved for marriage. You become emotionally connected with a person when that happens, and you become soul tied. I couldn't even think straight. The more I gave myself to him, the more I lost another part of me, who I was. I had changed into someone that I didn't like, all in my quest for love. Women, you have to stop giving yourself to every man looking for love. That's what I was doing; there was a hole in my soul, a void.

Do you understand what I'm saying? I know you all can relate to what I'm saying. I really didn't know God as Father, and I was so bitter with my own father. I just took the next substitute. I didn't have a father there to teach me, to show me true love, and to show me how a man is supposed to treat his wife or a woman. I know things would have been different in my life if I had seen the proper example. Please, if you are reading this book and you are facing the same situation or maybe similar, please, think about my life and what I went through. God loves you more than any man can. Just cry out to Him, and He will come to you. Remember, love gives. God already gave you the greatest gift, and that gift is His only begotten Son.

Chapter 2

The Example I Saw

My mother had gotten pregnant with her third child, and she was already living with her boyfriend, who was abusive even before they got married (my stepdad), when she married him. Who was going to take a woman that already had two children, when during that time it was an embarrassment to be pregnant and not be married? Well, my mother married him. The marriage was very abusive. I would sit and watch him beat my mom for hours, and then he would beat my sister and me. He was always sorry, but he never changed. I watched this for years, and it set me up to attract the same kind of person. My mom was teaching me that this was okay. Just stay, and maybe one day he will stop beating you. I used to hate my stepdad. I needed him to be a father to me, and it didn't matter to me that he wasn't my biological father. I just needed a dad to step in right on time, and he wasn't willing to do that. He saw his dad abuse his mom, and he did the same thing to his wife. What I learned after I grew up is that you can't give someone what you don't have. You have to love yourself first. The Bible says in Luke 10:27, "And he answered, You shall love the Lord your GOD with all your heart, and with all your soul, and with all your strength, and with all your mind, and your neighbor as yourself." If you don't love yourself first, then how can you love anyone else? You can't put your husband, boyfriend, or whomever before yourself. That's what I did, you see. I didn't have an earthly father teaching me or directing me how a man should treat a woman. I just followed the pattern that was set before me.

I saw my stepdad physically, verbally, and emotionally abuse my mom, so I ended up picking a man just like that. I truly believe that, in most cases, if more men would start being there for their daughters and sons, there would be fewer cases of domestic violence, child abuse, and prostitution, if the men would start raising their daughters. It doesn't matter if you are a stepdad, a foster dad, or an adoptive dad. (That's my opinion.) A mother is important to the development of her child, but a father is no less important. We need our fathers just like we need our mothers. You see, if my stepdad had treated me like I was a daughter and treated my mom like she was his wife and not his possession, I believe that things between him and my mother would have ended differently. Definitely things between him and me while I was growing up would have been different. It doesn't matter if you are a stepdad, which is a dad that steps in just in time. Most young girls just want you to love them and treat them just as if you were their biological father. You see, my stepdad was severely over protective, and we had a very bad relationship. He was very abusive to me and my sister, who weren't his biological children. His whole family, especially his nieces and nephews, treated us really badly. They always let us know that he wasn't our biological father, and that really hurt me. It damaged me and set me on the road called rejection. I wanted to be loved. My stepdad and my mom ended up divorcing after twenty-five years of marriage, when I was grown. My stepdad and I have a good relationship now. He became a Christian and a totally different person. Of course, everyone is different toward me now because they grew up. I forgave them for how they treated me; I had to because the only way that you can heal is to forgive. My Pops, which is what I call him, and I have a decent relationship. He realized a lot of his mistakes, and I wish that he could have changed them before I was an adult. But like the saying goes, you can't cry over spilt milk; you just have to keep moving and forgive.

Well, anyway, when my boyfriend left, I was left alone with God to get my life back on track. By the time he came back, I had repented and got back in right standing with God, but this was one of the hardest things that I ever had to do. I really loved this young man, but when it came down to it, I had to choose to follow God. I broke up with him. I was still in love with him, but I had to put things in the right perspective. I put God back in first place. We are still friends to this day. He accepted Christ into his life, and I really believe that if he had accepted Christ earlier, things would have been different between us. Like I said earlier, he had a lot of potential, but at that time in our life, we were going in different directions. He was more concerned about what he wanted. This young man is a wonderful guy, and I praise God that he is a Christian now. He got stationed in Germany for a few years and came back, and by this time everything was different in my life. I had met someone else and was moving on with my life.

I have to be honest. I met this young man, Minister R.W., while I was still on the rebound, and I just wanted a man that was a Christian, someone I thought that would be going in the same direction that I was going. I was never in love with him. I just convinced myself that this was the right thing to do, and so I played the role. You see, I was still in love with my ex-boyfriend; I thought about him all the time. I was on the rebound, and you should never get into a relationship with someone else if you aren't over your ex. You start lying to yourself and to the individual that you are trying to start a new relationship with. I went from one extreme to the next. I dated an unsaved man; now I was dating a super spiritual minister. I thought for sure this man would be right, because he was a Christian and a well-known preacher and prophet. Oh, was I wrong! He moved from up north to go to a college in South Carolina. I was getting my life back on track. My former boyfriend and I stayed friends, and everything was getting together in my life. I was in a new church; I felt like this was my new start. I learned that one of the consequences for my sin was that I had to give up the person that I had put in the place of God. It wasn't easy, but I did it. The Bible says in Exodus 20:3-5, "Thou shalt have no other gods before me. Thou shalt not make unto thee any graven image, or any likeness of any thing that is in heaven above, or that is in the earth beneath, or that is in the water under the earth: Thou shalt not bow down thyself to them, nor serve them: for I the Lord thy GOD am a jealous God, visiting the iniquity of the fathers upon the children unto the third and fourth generation of them that hate me." God must be first in our lives.

Chapter 3

The Valentine's Banquet

In 1988, our church was having a Valentine's Day banquet in another city, but I didn't go. I stayed at the church to baby-sit the kids of the parents who wanted to go to the banquet. The minister went to the banquet, and he had come back to the church afterwards. This is where it began. He said hello to me and asked me why I didn't go to the banquet. I said that no one had asked me to go. Then he replied, "I started to ask you." I said, "Well, you should have." From that point on, my life began to change. We started talking on the phone. He would say stuff like, "I didn't come to South Carolina to get a wife, but if that's what God has for me, then I'll take it." We would talk about everything, and then eventually, we started dating.

Let me interject a sidebar. Ladies, there is a saying that everything that glitters isn't always gold, and that was true in this situation. The young man was raised in church, but his insides were corrupt, full of dead men's bones. You know how you can be raised in Church, but just be going through the motions. That's how this young man was. He was very gifted, and you know that the Bible says in Romans

11:29, "For the gifts and the calling of God are without repentance." What that means to me is that you can be gifted and have a calling on your life but not really be a saved Christian. The Bible says in Matthew 7:21-23, "Not everyone that saith unto me Lord, Lord, shall enter into the Kingdom of heaven; but he that doeth the will of my Father which is in heaven. Many will say to me in that day, Lord, Lord, have we not prophesied in thy name? And in thy name have cast out devils? And in thy name done many wonderful works? And then will I profess unto them; I never knew you depart from me, ye that work iniquity." What this text is saying is that many will say when the Lord returns, "Lord, did I not prophesy in your name?" But God is going to say, "Depart from me, you worker of iniquity; I never knew you."

I learned this Scripture passage in my dealings with Minister R.W. You have to live the life that you preach about. You may be a gifted preacher, but you must live the same words that you preach. He started out with a list of requirements from the beginning of the relationship, all these dos and don'ts. When we sat down to talk, it was as if we had a meeting at the Oval Office, and he was the commander in chief. I really don't know why I agreed to all of his orders. I guess I was man desperate. I was no different than when I was in my first relationship; I was still wounded. I just was in a different type of relationship. I still had a hole in my soul, and I really didn't deal with it. I went from one extreme to the next. I wouldn't allow God to heal me. I wanted to keep the pain, the resentment, and the unforgivingness for my father all on the inside. You cannot get with someone who starts out with a list of rules; remember, you are already an adult. You need a mate, not a parent. Here are some of the rules that the commander in chief had given me. I had to look good at all times, because I was representing him and he was very much into appearance. I had to look a certain way, talk a certain way, and act a certain way. Ladies, these are all signs of an abuser. They start trying to control every part of your life. They can start with small, little things, like asking what time you are going to be home or telling you that you need to be home at a certain time. We often say, "That's sweet; he is just concerned about me." Often times we just blow those signs off and allow the individual to dictate to us and control us. I allowed him to control me and dictate to me, and I remained silent.

We ended up dating four years before we were married, because he was still in college. Well, he ended up getting sick, and he had to withdraw from college to go back up north. I really can't say that I was in love with him, initially. I eventually began to talk myself into believing that I was in love with him. I had more compassion for him. Because of all the abuse that he had gone through, we had something in common. We were both survivors of child abuse, rape, etc. Looking back, I know that I wasn't truly over my ex-boyfriend, but this man was a Christian. He was not only a Christian; he was a minister as well. I didn't want to hurt God anymore, and I thought that this would please God. Like I said earlier, I went from one extreme to the other. I dated a man who wasn't saved, and then I started dating a man who was not just saved, but super saved, if I can use that terminology. He was super spiritual. What I have learned in my life is that we have to be well-balanced. We have to be balanced in every area. We can't walk around here being spooky Christians and running people away from Christ; in so doing, we become poor representations of Christ.

Anyway, I stayed in the relationship in spite of how I felt. I felt like I heard God say that this man was the one for me, but I should have checked his background. I should have talked to people who really knew him and how he really was. I believe it has to go farther than that: you really have to watch a person's life, not what he says out of his mouth. The life has to and should line up with what he is saying and proclaiming, but in this case, he was living a double life. He had his own demons to deal with, but instead of really focusing on his own problems, he was severely hard on everyone else. He preached a fire and brimstone message but lived a double life. Preachers, you must be first partakers of the messages you preach. You must first live the life. Don't preach on something that you haven't overcome or walked out yourself, which is exactly what he did. He preached a message that he wasn't a first partaker of.

Chapter 4

He Said I Was His Wife

He said that he didn't come down south to get a wife, but if that's what God wanted to do, then he was fine with it. What I found out about this young man was that he had a private life up north that he had not told me about. God revealed some things to me concerning his life that were similar to my life. For example, we were both survivors of child abuse, rape, and molestation. He was raped and molested by men; I was molested and raped by both men and a young lady. I felt sorry for him, because I knew how it felt to be abused in every way. I could relate to his pain; it's a pain that only God and time can heal. Feeling sorry for someone does not make a marriage.

Let me get back to when we started dating; this was while he was still in college. One of my first signs that he was an abuser was that he wanted me to dress a certain way to make him look good. At first I really didn't think anything of it. He said that he wanted to take me shopping, and so we went to the mall. He bought me these nice shoes and all my accessories to go with a new dress that was given to me. I thought that it was sweet of him. Then, after he bought me those things, he started giving me orders about not letting my mother wear what he had bought for me, and when my mother saw my things and wanted to wear them, he jumped all over her about wanting to wear my things eventually. I have always been a liberal person, and he tried to change that about me. He was so very rude to my mom; he jumped all over her and told her that he bought those things for me and only me. He really made her upset because of the way he spoke to her and disrespected her. He didn't have to do that, and I shouldn't have allowed him to speak to my mom that way. That was my first sign that something was not right with him, and although I should have broken up with him from that point, I didn't. Then, as our relationship progressed, he always insisted that I look my best, because it was all about me making him look good. He came from a poor, extremely dysfunctional, and abusive family, just like my family. He was picked on a lot, and he valued anything that he received, because he was used to being without.

Our relationship continued. We prayed a lot together, fasted a lot, and he wasn't trying to get me into bed, because he had desires for men. He had never been with a woman, so that wasn't a struggle for him. Oftentimes he would tell me that he wanted to let me know, just in case anyone came to me concerning him and his struggle with homosexuality. He would tell me that a certain young man that was on campus had tried to have sex with him, or had come on to him, or had touched him in an inappropriate way. He would tell me that nothing happened, and it was always men trying after him. He never told me that he was hitting on some of these young men. Like I said, he was a Christian, or should I say that he confessed to be a Christian. But there are a lot of men and women claiming that they are Christians who are not living a Christ-like lifestyle: that's what

The Battered Preacher's Wife

the word Christian means. I never had to worry about him trying to have sex with me, because he wasn't tempted by me. There was no struggle in that regard. He told me that he had been abused in every way by his mother. She had knocked his front teeth out of his mouth by kicking him into a table. She tried to set him on fire. She was very abusive to him and his siblings, and he had a lot of permanent scars on his body and in pictures to show. He said that one of his mom's many boyfriends had sodomized him when he was a child, and then an older boy had raped and sodomized him for a number of years. This was all he knew, and so he was battling with his desire to be with men, because that's what he was introduced to. It became familiar to him. I didn't condemn him. I understood him, because I was a survivor of child abuse. I was raped and molested by my step uncle and others that were adults, so I felt his pain. I zoned in on the fact that he had been through so much, and I put his pain before my own unresolved issues. He wasn't completely honest with me about his struggles. He never took ownership for his actions; he always put the blame on someone else. The first step to knowing that you have a problem is admitting it, and that's what his problem was: he just wouldn't admit that he was doing something that was attracting this type of attention. Like I said earlier, I never condemned him, but he used me as a shield to hide behind who he really wanted to be.

    I remember the first time he showed signs that he could potentially be violent. It was about three months into our relationship. He had gotten upset about something. I can't remember what set him off, but anyway, I was trying to get him to calm down. I had a purse with a strap on my shoulder, and he pushed the purse so hard that it hit me. He kept telling me to get away from him. I was in shock. I know it seems like it was a small thing, but I knew in that moment that he could possibly be violent. He had such a rage in his eyes, and ladies, if you have ever been abused; you know what I'm talking about. Pay attention to the small things. He was very apologetic after he calmed down. I accepted his apology, but I told my mother what had happened. She told my ex-boyfriend what had happened, and like I said earlier, we remained friends. He was home that weekend, and he talked to me concerning R.W. hitting me with the purse. His words were, "If he gets that angry to hit you with a purse, what's going to stop him from hitting you?" I replied that he wouldn't do that. He still tried to warn me, but I wouldn't listen. I thought he was trying to get me back. He even tried to give me examples of people who had showed signs of abuse before they married someone, but I wouldn't listen. I regretted that day. How I wish I would have listened. He was just trying to look out for me.

Ladies, you might already be in a relationship. If you are noticing some of the signs that I have mentioned, then you need to get out of the relationship. Stop it before it gets started, because it's all downhill from that point. The first time a man can hit you or push you without any consequences, it makes it easier for him to hit you, push you, or verbally abuse you the next time.

That was another sign that he was an abuser in every sense of the word. I stayed in the relationship and excused his violent behavior. He was still preaching and trying to control me in every way, but because we weren't married, he could only do so much. Things in our relationship continued to change. He was very demanding, and everything had to go his way. He was very matter of fact. If I did anything that he didn't like, he was going to let me know. If I laughed too much, talked too much, or did something that didn't line up with his set of rules, he was going to correct me. I lost myself trying to obey his orders. Then he got sick and had to move back up north. Shortly after that, he called me and asked me to marry him. I said yes. I moved up north with a young lady from the church in December 1991. He showed more signs of abuse when I moved there. We got into an argument, and he took his engagement ring back and pushed me out of his apartment door. I was in shock. He pushed me. That should have been enough right there. God was giving me all the signs not to marry him, but I felt like I was too far into it to back out. It was only two months before the wedding. He calmed down, apologized to me, and gave me the ring back. What was wrong with me; why did I take the ring back? I just believed I couldn't back out now. So many people prophesied (to speak as if divinely inspired) that we were supposed to be together that I thought it was God who had brought us together.

What I've learned is that God can give you a blessing, and it's up to you how you handle it. I also learned that the devil can set you up with someone who looks like a blessing from God, but who really is an Ishmael. Before Isaac came Ishmael (Genesis 17:19). Isaac was the son of promise to Abraham and Sarah, but when they didn't believe, Ishmael came about as a result of Sarah's disbelief through her handmaiden Hagar. This was not God's original plan. God promised Abraham Isaac. I missed my Isaac the first time, dealing with a counterfeit. The minister had a lot of deep-seated issues that he was unwilling to let go. When God sends you a blessing, the Bible says that the blessings of the Lord make you rich and add no sorrow (Proverbs 10:22). A blessing from God doesn't try to kill you, but compliments you. You can fast and pray and have all the preachers or pastors in the world lay hands on you for deliverance. But after the fasting, praying, and laying on of hands, you have to live, and you have to begin to walk in the deliverance. For example, if you have an addiction, until you are strong enough you should not put yourself in the places or around the people that will cause you to fall back into the thing that you are struggling with. His struggle was homosexuality, which was the root cause, I believe, for his violence toward me.

We ended up having another big blow up over the phone. He told me that he was putting me on the bus back to South Carolina. My roommate called the pastor, because he was screaming and yelling at me on the phone. I talked to the pastor, and he said that he could not put me on the bus to South Carolina because he didn't bring me up north. We worked out our differences and moved on with the wedding. I would do a lot of walking at that time. I would think to myself, *I shouldn't do this*, but then I thought, *he would never hit me. He's just under a lot of stress, and he's a well-known preacher and prophet*. Women, we often make excuses for our men, because somewhere in there is our desperation for a husband, or the fact that we just settle and think we can't do any better. Often times it's because of low self-esteem, which is what I had. I believe that it was God's will to bless my marriage, but my husband didn't want to submit his will or struggles totally to the Lord. You have to remember that the devil can send you someone that acts like a real Christian, but when you get into the relationship, you begin to see who he really is. The way he acted in church didn't add up with how he treated me.

I worked for a woman who was a pastor. She was like a spiritual mother to me. I confided in her about what he was doing to me, and her words to me were, "If he's doing these things to you, like pushing you, screaming at you, arguing with you, and controlling

The Battered Preacher's Wife

you now, then what do you think he's going to do when you get married?" She told me I didn't have to marry him, because she felt that he was going to be abusive. I heard what she said, but I thought he would never hit me. I thought he was just too saved and too well-known as a preacher to hit me. I was so wrong.

We got down to the day before the wedding. My friend had picked me up, and he was going to pick Minister R.W., my fiancé, up from work. He told me that I should not mention anything to him about all the things that were going wrong, because he knew that we were both under a lot of stress. You know that, when you're preparing to get married, it seems like everything goes wrong. Well, I didn't listen. I had to ask him something, because all of my family was coming from South Carolina, and his apartment phone wasn't on. I started questioning him about why the telephone was off. I told him that my family needed to get in touch with me, and they couldn't do that because the phone wasn't on. In that moment, he just went off, and he started grabbing me. I was sitting in the front seat on the passenger side. He was holding my hands behind my back from the back seat, pulling my hair, and telling me I needed to shut up. My friend was telling him to let me go because all his co-workers were watching. Eventually I was able to get myself loose from him. Well, what was wrong with me? We separated for the remainder of the day, and I didn't see him until the wedding rehearsal. At that moment, I knew I shouldn't have gone through with it. He apologized for what he had done to me with tears and everything, and that was it. I didn't call off the wedding. I knew I should have, but I thought he would never hit me. He was a preacher, a man of God.

Chapter 5

The Wedding

We got married on March 22, 1992. The wedding was beautiful, the most beautiful wedding that many people said that they had ever seen. Some people said that they had never been at a wedding like ours. He wrote a song to me, and I came in on that song. I sang a song to him; we danced and praised God like we were at a church service. We had a gospel celebrity to sing at our wedding. It was a wedding that was second to none; people cried and rejoiced. Well, when the wedding was over and we were leaving the reception, my now husband was calling me. I was busy talking to someone else at the time, and I told him I would be there in a minute. He yelled at me and demanded that I come to him at that moment. I couldn't believe he was yelling at me right there in church, while I was still in my wedding gown. I thought, *That was uncalled for*. I guess I thought that once we were married I could change him; I thought I could help him get the healing and deliverance he so desperately needed.

Women, a lot of us think that we can cure or heal a man from an addiction or from abuse or whatever the case may be. Healing has to begin from within the individual. He must recognize that he has a problem and seek God for true deliverance. You can want a person to be healed, delivered, or set free, but he must recognize the need for help. Our wedding night was difficult for him. He just couldn't be intimate, so he had to wait until morning and put some music on to get in the mood. I knew then that this was a marriage of convenience and that he really didn't love me the way I needed to be loved. This was another sign that I should not have married him. He married me to cover up who he really was or who he really wanted to be. He used me as a shield, someone for him to hide behind so he could do what he wanted.

Our marriage was okay for the first six months. And after that, everything went downhill; my life became a living nightmare. We went to a friend's wedding, where I later found out that he had been somehow involved with some of the guys that were there in a sexual way, and so his whole attitude changed towards me once we left the wedding. This was the first day that he hit me with his hand. It was on a Saturday in October. I can't remember what set him off, but when we started arguing, he grabbed me with a necklace I was wearing. He didn't like it when I talked back to him, and then he slapped me in the face so that I fell back on the bed. I was in shock; I was in disbelief. I just lay there on the bed thinking, *I can't believe he just slapped me.* I thought, *if you loved someone or even cared about them, how could you do that to them?* He went into the living room, and he began to cry. He could cry very easily. Then I felt sorry for him. So I went in the living room, and I comforted him. He said, "I have never hit a woman, and I'm so sorry." He said, "This is not me; I don't know why I did that." I accepted his apology, but it was like another person stepped in from that day on. From that first slap, it became easier for him to hit me.

He lost his job shortly after we got married, because he was taking off from work all the time. If he didn't feel like going to work, he would call off. I asked him if he had time to be taking off from work, and he said that he had enough time to take off from work. Then the day came when he got fired. When he got fired, he became very depressed, and he took out his frustration on me. I thought I was living at home again. When I was growing up, every Saturday my mom and stepdad would get into an argument, and every Saturday it seemed to be an argument which resulted in a fight. Once an abuser hits you, it becomes easier for him to do it again. The minister slapped me, pulled my hair, and dragged me; it didn't matter to him. The first slap came six months after we were married. Then he went from slapping me to punching me or choking me.

Let me tell you a little bit about my health. When I was born, I had problems with my lungs, and I was kept in the hospital for some weeks after my birth. They said I was asthmatic, and I grew up very sickly, having asthma attacks quite frequently, being in and out of the hospital many times. I was even in intensive care. I was on a medication back then called theodur (theophylline) for asthma. Doctors diagnosed me as being a severe asthmatic, having sinusitis, bronchitis, and allergies. I was always in the hospital, and the minister knew this: he used my sickness to torture me more. He could fight me for hours, it didn't matter. It was like he loved to fight. It was like he turned into a monster. The more he fought me, the stronger he got.

I remember the first time I left him for one night; he cried and was so sorry that I went back. He always promised he wouldn't do it again. He couldn't find a job, and he took it out on me. Then, when he would get a job, he wouldn't keep it for very long before he was fired, and so he took it out on me. He would tell me that the apartment had to stay clean, the dishes had to be done, and everything had to be in its proper place. I had a job working in a daycare as a preschool teacher, and then I was promoted to assistant director. God had given me favor with my boss. Although I was going to church and my husband and I were both in the ministry, he was fighting me; he was verbally, physically, and mentally abusive. I continued to play the role of a happy preacher's wife, but deep down inside, I was dying. He was killing me in every area. Nothing I did was ever good enough for him. The arguments would be about stuff that was so small. I remember one night we got in to it, and I was talking back. There are a lot of men, even preachers and pastors, who believe women just need to keep quiet and not say anything back. They look at it as a sign of disrespect, and they are not going to have that. He started arguing with me, and because I had a strong personality, I wasn't going to let him keep talking to me like I was dirt or treating me like I was dirt. He would grab my mouth and twist it around. He would say things like, "Since you won't shut up, then I will shut you up." Then he threw me around in the kitchen. I was saying, "Jesus," and he said, "Don't call Jesus now; you should have been calling Him before you opened up your mouth." He treated me like I was less than an animal. I knew people that treated their pets better than he was treating me. Then he took me into the living room. I was fighting him, but this was over an hour later. Remember I told you earlier that I was a severe asthmatic. I was wheezing really badly, and he started choking me. This night I thought I was going to die. I had no more strength in me, and I began to apologize to him for whatever I had done to him. I couldn't understand why he was beating me and choking me like this. I wanted everything to be right if I was going to see God in that moment. I was blacking out, because he had a death grip on my throat. I really thought he was going to kill me, and he was in the position to do so. I was wheezing really badly, and he said, "Do you need your inhaler?" I said, "Yes," and then he started choking me again. But all of a sudden, he let me go. He asked me if I wanted to leave, and I said, "Yes." I ran outside barely dressed and went to his godfather's house. I looked a mess, and I told the godfather what had happened. He called the cops and took me back home to get some clothes. The cops came and questioned me about what happened. I told them that the minister was fighting me. They asked me if he hit me, and I said, "Yes." They asked me, "With an open hand or closed?" I said, "With an open hand." The cops said that we needed to separate. R.W. didn't offer to leave, so his godfather took me to a women's shelter. The minister called me in the room and had one of the church mothers on the phone trying to stop me from leaving. I explained to her that R.W. was fighting me, and I couldn't stay with him.

It is so common for someone to tell you to stay and hope for the best. I was supposed to be a Christian, and not only that, I was married to a well-known preacher who was preaching all over the city and was an associate minister at our church. How and why was this happening to me? I remember times of him taking his drink and just throwing it right in my face. He did all kinds of things to me. I left, but I would always end up coming back. Well, even though I saw my mother go through this, I didn't believe in divorce, because the church frowned on that, so I stayed with him. He was a well-known preacher, and he was abusing me and still preaching. I didn't tell anyone until it got out that he was fighting me. My neighbor started calling the cops every time she would hear me over there screaming. I was so embarrassed. I could not believe that this was happening to me. The abuse continued to escalate, and I contemplated killing him.

I felt like I was in a hole, and I couldn't get out. I would pray and ask God to take the thoughts away, but there's a saying that if you beat up on a dog long enough, he will turn and bite you. Women, I really understand all the rationalizing and making excuses. One of the excuses that we use is, "I don't believe in divorce." Well, you must believe in letting someone kill you, because that is what's happening. You're not only letting him control you, but you are slowly losing yourself physically, emotionally, and psychologically. And you lose yourself every day that you stay and play that role, trying to make that preacher or pastor look good. You constantly have to fight against him. Especially if you have a calling or are anointed to preach or do anything better than he does, then he has to compete with you. That was the hardest thing for me. How do you say you love me if you are jealous of me? Women, if that man can't help you be a better person, then you just need to let him be, let him go. A real man of God will support you and push you to be and become a better person; he is secure in who he is. The secret rule when you are a battered preacher or pastor's wife, because your husband is in the forefront, is to play the role of happy wife. So many people are looking at you; they are watching everything that you do, especially when he's up preaching. They look at you to see how you respond to him while he's preaching. If you don't support him while he is in the public eye, then when you get home, you are going to pay for embarrassing him. You are definitely going to get beat down, because you are making him look bad. I remember it was always a fight or argument about something.

The Battered Preacher's Wife

Like I said earlier, image was everything to him, because he came from a poor family. Also, he was looked down on and teased by many, because he was a short man. I always had to make him look good. If we went out to visit friends, and if I laughed too much, he would tell me, and I quote, "Avril, that's enough." He tried to control me in every area. When men, or people for that matter, are insecure, they try to make themselves feel better by trying to belittle you and make you look or feel like you are beneath them.

We stayed legally married for six years, but I left him several times. I can remember early on in our marriage, before I had my daughters; I went to South Carolina for a visit. I stayed about a week. I was tired of the abuse. He did everything to stop me from leaving. It was cold, so I had gloves on. He just kept arguing with me until I had gotten so angry that I was trying to push the door, and I pushed the glass panels on the door. Both of my hands went through the glass, breaking them. I thank God that I had my gloves on, because my wrists were not cut. He left me alone, and I went to South Carolina. I came back a week later, and when I tried to lie down in the bed, I couldn't. I said to him, "Who was in this bed?" God had just revealed to me that he had someone in my bed. I said, "Someone was in this bed, and you are going to tell me." At that moment he confessed to having an affair with another man, but he said he didn't go all the way. What he was saying was that they didn't have intercourse, because he got sick when the man tried, but in my mind, it is still wrong. He still had an affair, and the thing that hurt the most was that he had it with another man in the bed where I slept. He didn't even have enough respect to do it somewhere else; that's just wrong.

At this time, he was preparing to receive his ordination. He was being promoted to an elder in the church, and I had helped him with his studies. I should have said something to the pastor, but I didn't. I just kept it all inside, and when he touched me, I felt so dirty. I can't begin to describe the pain I was in. When we went to the Church of God in Christ Convocation, and he received his ordination as an elder, he should not have received it. He was not right or ready for it, and I was just as much to blame, because I remained silent. I didn't say anything. I stayed married to him while the abuse continued, and when he preached in the city or wherever he had an engagement, I made him look good by supporting him and wearing that fake smile. I felt like I was the biggest hypocrite ever.

Then, in 1994, I found out I was pregnant. I guess I thought that if I had a child, then maybe he would stop fighting me, and maybe he would want me. I was totally wrong. I always told him that he was making me suffer for everyone that hurt him. I was a high-risk pregnancy because of my chronic asthma. Well, I was very sick, and I ended up in and out of the hospital my whole pregnancy. While I was in my first trimester, they told me that if I was going to lose my baby during this stage, there was nothing they could do. I would have to make it to the second trimester. I kept having asthma attacks, and I really didn't want to lose my baby. I had to catch the bus to work, and I would pray, *Please, God, don't let me lose my baby.* The minister wasn't working at this time. I was under so much stress. Then there were times I had to walk home, because I didn't have enough money to catch the bus, while he was at home lying on the couch doing nothing, having his pregnant wife taking care of him. I was paying the rent, trying to keep the lights on, and putting food on the table, while he just lay around doing nothing. When he had a job, he always took off, and then he would always get fired.

During my first trimester, he got angry with me and started fighting me while I was pregnant. He punched me in the stomach, and I said, "Oh, my baby!" He claimed that he didn't do that, but I will never forget it. He would tell me when he wasn't working that I needed to give him my paycheck so that he could feel like he was a part, and he would disperse the money on the bills. I told him, "How you feel like you are a part is by going out and getting a job." He really got angry with me. He started working for about three months, when I was about six months pregnant. When I had my daughter, he had a job, and one of the sisters from the church had come to visit me in the hospital. She said to me, "I need to talk to you about your husband." You see, they worked on the same job. She told me that they were talking about firing him, because he had been calling off from work so much. She wanted me to try and talk to him, because she knew that I was off on maternity leave. Well, how was I going to talk to him? He wouldn't listen to anything that I had to say. I tried to talk to him, but it didn't do any good. He ended up getting fired. While I was off on maternity leave, my boss paid me my regular pay; otherwise, I don't know how we would have made it. It was nothing but the favor of God. I will never forget you, F.C.

The minister didn't keep a job for one whole year during six years of marriage, and he didn't go for one whole year without hitting me. After he hit me during my first trimester, he didn't hit me anymore. I had six months of no hitting, and I thought that maybe this would work. Well, I was wrong. He started back fighting me a short time after I had my daughter. Why did he start back hitting me? I don't know for what reason. He was very dramatic. I remember him recording a tape saying that he saw all that I had endured going through labor, and he vowed never to hit me again. It was just a waste of breath and air. He might have meant what he said in that moment, but it was just words. I remember one time he hit me about a year before I had my daughter, and I left him for about a month or so. But I always let the church people prophesy me back with him.

Pastors or leaders in the church, you have an obligation to protect the women, not send them back to be further beaten or even killed. That's what I let the church and the church folks do to me. I let them persuade me to go back, because God doesn't want us to get divorced. God doesn't want you to let a man kill you either. The Bible says in Ephesians 5:25, "Husbands, love your wives, even as Christ also loved the church, and gave himself for it." God did not tell you to beat your wife or abuse her in any way. I was not only beaten physically, but I was also beaten emotionally. Stop sending our daughters to be slaughtered, men of God. Women, I'm telling you as a woman of God to get out before it's too late. You can't help your husband or boyfriend. Even if it's a man being abused by a woman, and there are cases where women are abusive to their husbands, you must first help yourself by getting out of that negative environment, because it's very toxic. It's a slow killer. You have to put a value on you.

I remember that after I had my daughter there was always something for him to fight with me about. I think he would make up things to fight about. He wanted a man. Nothing I did was good enough, and he didn't sleep with me much anyway, maybe once a month or after he physically abused me. After an abuser abuses, he always wants to try to fix the victim.

I remember the time that he started fighting me in front of my daughter. You see, when he got angry, something else stepped in him and it controlled him. If someone treated him wrong at the church,

The Battered Preacher's Wife

he would come home and take it out on me. My daughter was about a year and a half. He started fussing, because he was mad. About what, I don't remember. I was trying to get him to calm down, but he wouldn't. Then my daughter came in and said, "Pray," and that stopped him for the moment. Then somehow he started back up. It was like I could see the face of rage in his eyes, and nothing could stop him from coming for me. We ended up in our bedroom (we had a one bedroom apartment). He grabbed me and started wrestling with me like I was a man. I was saying, "Please stop, our daughter is right there." She put herself in the way, and she got knocked down. She was crying, and that still wasn't enough to make him stop. Then he slapped me on the right side of my face, because he was left-handed, and my ear popped like a gun firing. I screamed, "Oh, my ear!" Then he stopped at that moment. I couldn't hear well, and everything sounded far away. Then I heard the neighbor upstairs coming running down the stairs to check on me. He was knocking on the door as if he was trying to knock it down. He said, "Man, what's going on; you need to stop beating your wife! It's not right; you are supposed to be a preacher, a man of God." He said, "You hit her hard, so hard that I heard it upstairs in my apartment." Then the minister said, "Everything is okay." He had nothing to say but that everything was okay. Everything was not okay. My ear was hurting so bad, and so he tried to fix it. He tried to put a cold cloth on it, and then water got in my ear. I can't tell you why I didn't call the cops. He would come in the bed and always wanted to be intimate; I felt like I was a piece of trash. I couldn't sink any lower. I was totally distraught. I ended up going to the doctor the next day, because the pain was so bad and I couldn't hear well. The doctor examined me, and she said that my eardrum was split from top to bottom. This was my opportunity to confess to her and report that I was a victim of domestic violence. I could tell her that my husband was beating me on a consistent basis, but I didn't. I just asked the doctor what could cause this. She said, "Too much fluid built up in the ear, a hit to the ear, etc." When the opportunity presented itself for me to tell someone, I didn't. I just played it off like it was a sinus problem, because as I stated earlier, I had sinus problems. I will never forget that when I was walking back to work I kept saying, *he split my ear drum.* It took a while for my ear to heal, but it did. I still have problems with that ear; to this day my ear still bothers me.

I can recall the time that he was angry because I told him that he needed to get a job and keep one, and that started a fight. He got on top of me and started grabbing my hair and yanking my hair, and he yanked my hair so hard with both of his hands that I couldn't move my neck. It was stuck; I had to go to a chiropractor. He said that I had a herniated disc in my neck and that I had to go to physical therapy for a very long time. Then recently, in 2002, I had to go to physical therapy again because discs seven and eight had deteriorated down to the nerve as a result of the injury. I had to wear a neck brace, and I had to go to physical therapy the second time. Until this day, I still have the neck brace, because my neck bothers me at certain times. The pain is always there. I have just learned to live with the pain.

The word about the minister beating me had gotten to the pastor, and he started trying to counsel us. He even came to the house several times, trying to help us, but the minister would disrespect the pastor and say that he wasn't fighting by himself. He said that I was doing something to make him be violent. Well, the pastor told him that he could not preach for a certain time until he stopped fighting me. Although the pastor didn't make me stop preaching and held

R.W. responsible, that only made things worse. The minister told the pastor that I should have to stop preaching along with him. His reason was that it took two to fight. The pastor asked him who hit first. It was always him. And the pastor said, "Well, I'm not holding her for trying to defend herself." He would fight me even more when he couldn't preach. He said that I ruined his life. He said that it was my fault that this had happened to him. If I had kept silent, he would have still been able to beat me, fool around with men, and still preach.

I remember I stopped going to church on Friday nights, because the pastor would allow the ministers and missionaries, which is what they called the women in the C.O.G.I.C. who were in the ministry, about fifteen minutes to bring a sermonette. The pastor called me up to preach one Friday night, and my husband looked at me with a look of, *just wait until I get you home*. When we got home, there was always an argument or something, because I had caused him to be sat down. It was not my fault. It was his fault. He chose to beat me. Because I internalized everything that he accused me of, I stopped going to church on Fridays so that the pastor wouldn't call me up to preach and so that I wouldn't have to fight with R.W. when I went home.

I remember things getting so bad that I had got to the point that I was going to pawn my wedding rings, purchase a gun, and kill him. I told the pastor that he should try to talk to R.W., because I was at the point of killing him. Nothing was done, and he was fighting me again. He was sitting on top of me, hitting me, and I told him that if I got up off this chair and out that door, then I was going to get a gun and kill him. I couldn't take it anymore. He began to hold me down and tried to reason with me. He didn't let me get out of the door, and I calmed down. But nothing changed. I resisted the thoughts of killing him. I went to counseling, and that helped me to deal with my thoughts. Women, look at my life and all the suffering that I endured and am still enduring for the rest of my life or until God heals my body. You have to place a value on you; you have to place value on your life. You have to place value on your child or children and their well-being.

The abuse continued, and it got to a point that I had to get a protection from abuse order against him (restraining order) for the second time. We separated. He could not come within one hundred feet of me, and he had to go to anger management. He was obedient to the court order and went to counseling, but it didn't help him. We were separated for about a year, and somewhere in there I let people talk me into going back with him. I thought that the year was enough time for him to change, but it wasn't. He would always be sweet when I came back. For about three months, he would treat me like a queen. I was the best thing since sliced bread. Once we got back together, I got pregnant again. We went through what I like to call the honeymoon syndrome for about three months. While I was pregnant with this one, he didn't physically hit me, but he was verbally abusive. When we got back together, we sat down and had a long conversation. We were in our fourth year of marriage, and I told him that if he couldn't get himself together and not hit me, then after the fifth year, it was over. I told him that if he ever hit me again, that would be it. Well, I wanted a son, but I had a girl. Today I'm glad I had two beautiful daughters; in my opinion, it would have been much harder to explain to a boy about his father's sexuality. I can remember when my second daughter got sick; he wouldn't come to the hospital with me I had to go alone. My daughter ended up having to have her spine tapped; she was only three months old. They found out that my daughter had meningitis and she had to be hospitalized. She could have died, but he didn't care, everything was always about him. I didn't deserve that and neither did my daughter. I always had to take care of everything, and even when I was pregnant I worked almost until my due date. I had to drive to and from work, even though I shouldn't have been driving. I went to my doctor's appointments alone and when I didn't have a car or bus money I would have to walk where I needed to go. I always felt like the scum of the earth, and a husband is supposed to value you, and add value to your life. I was slowly dying.

We as women let the church people dictate to us that it's wrong to leave a husband. They say, "Just try not to get him angry. Try not to set him off, just be quiet." I tried everything: silence, fasting and praying, letting the preachers lay hands on the both of us, and going to marriage counseling. But it didn't work, because he believed that his sexuality was something that he had to struggle with for the rest of his life. I tried to tell him that the same God that you get up in the pulpit and preach about delivering others can deliver you and set you free, but he just didn't believe it. There was a constant battle in our home, because I needed my husband to love me, and he didn't. He would always find a man to befriend, and he would fall in love with him. I know what the Bible teaches about unnatural affections, but this was true. He became a mentor to this young man that was straight, and then he fell in love with him. He talked about him all the time, was overly involved in his life, and would take money from me and my children to give to him or help him. He bought into that spirit of homosexuality that is against nature itself, which is against the natural order of God, and I believe that's why he fought me so much. I am not condemning anyone, but I'm just quoting what I believe. There's no way possible for a man and a man or a woman and a woman to reproduce and multiply. That's what God said in Genesis 1:27-28: "So God created man in his own image, in the image of God created he him, male and female created he them. And God blessed them and God said unto them be fruitful and multiply and replenish the earth and subdue it." The same sexes can't reproduce. God has given everyone a choice. If this is what you choose to do, then it is your choice. But if you want to be free from any addiction or thing that has you bound, then the power of God is available, and you must put forth the effort to change. God is not going to do everything for you. For example, if you want to stop smoking, God is not going to come down from heaven and take the cigarette out of your hand. You have to put it down.

If my husband had been honest with me and told me that he wanted to be with a man, I would have left without a fight, because he had totally destroyed me and everything that was good and strong about me. I ended up finding out from so many men that were friends of ours that he had made passes at them and had said inappropriate things to them. My neighbors told me that he had all kinds of men coming in and out of the apartment when I wasn't there. How do you think I felt? I felt like I was worthless. Like I said, if you want to live your life like that, then that's your choice. But don't mess up someone else's life in the process.

I had gone to a conference, and I had been tired of fighting and everything that was going on. I asked God to show me the truth, and that's when everyone started coming out of the woodwork and telling me what R.W. was doing. If you ask God for the truth, He will show you the truth. R.W. would take my car to meet men, but

The Battered Preacher's Wife

he always claimed that someone tried to hurt him or rape him. I used to tell him, "If you want to be delivered from this, you need to stop going around it." I can remember when he got into a terrible state of depression, and remember earlier that I stated that his house had to be clean. Well, when he kept losing his jobs, he got depressed and wouldn't do anything. He started leaving clothes everywhere. I would go to work and leave him on the couch and come back and find him still on the couch. My oldest daughter was asthmatic and had been so sickly that she was put on disability. Because I didn't have my car then, I would have to carry her, her car seat, my things, and a nebulizer to the bus every morning, and he wouldn't help me. I was on my own. I felt so alone. An abuser always isolates you and makes you feel like no one cares about you. He would say, "Your family doesn't even care about you." These types of men major in making you feel alone and isolated, and at one point, I started to believe him. I was up north, and they were in South Carolina. He wasn't helping me; he was tearing me down bit by bit. I ended up injuring both the tendons and muscles in my left and right hand from carrying everything by myself and from him dragging me and pulling me by my wrists and my hands. I ended up wearing a semi-cast. I thought, *why did I give this man the power to abuse me?* I was looking for love, and when I asked him if he loved me after five years of hell, he said to me, and I quote: "I don't know what love is; I only know the love of my grandmother."

That's when I decided enough was enough. Why weren't a split ear drum, black eyes, scratches, bruises, blows to my head, a herniated disk in my neck, and my daughter being knocked down while he was fighting me enough? I said to him, "Well, what have I been doing for these last ten years (four years dating him and six years married to him) of my life?" I guess I was wrong, too, because I didn't love him, either. I was still in love with my former boyfriend, and this young man just fit the part. I saw my stepdad abuse my mother, and my mother did the same thing. I didn't want my kids to follow my example, so I had to do something. I didn't want dysfunction to become normal to my children like it did to me. That's why I could stay, leave, and then come back as if he was going to change. He could have changed if he wanted it bad enough, but he didn't. I had to learn that God is my Father and that He can love me like no man can.

Chapter 6

The Final Blow

Here is what finally caused me to divorce him. Remember that I said when I came back from the almost year separation that if he couldn't keep his hands off me in five years, then that was it. Well, I ended up staying with him for one year above the five year mark. God had given me favor, and my cousin helped us to get a house to rent with the option to buy. We had two daughters now, and the one bedroom apartment was not going to work any longer. Once we moved into the house, it was supposed to be our fresh start. I said, "Look, please leave what you use to do in the old place, and respect me for the woman that I am. Allow me to be me." He agreed to the fresh start and all the things that I stated. We had a four bedroom, semidetached house with a full basement and a full bathroom. It was truly a blessing from God. God blessed us with furniture to fill it and everything. The minister had gotten another job. I had changed jobs. Everything was going good for about three months.

Then he started being friends with the man from the wedding. I stated earlier that the minister hit me for the first time in the first year of our marriage after we had come back from his wedding.

This man from the wedding was once heavy into the homosexual life, and he stepped out of the ministry to make it known that this was the life that he chose. Well, the young man and his wife were divorced, and he and R.W. the minister somehow became close to him, or drawn to him. I was very skeptical of the friendship, because everyone knew of his former lifestyle. In spite of my skepticism, they became close, and he embraced me as a friend. So I thought, *okay, maybe it will be okay.* Well, I was wrong. It would not be okay. It started that this young man, who had rededicated his life to the Lord, started slipping back into the things of the world, and then he started going to the clubs. So one night he called my husband and asked him if he could pick him up from a club, because he had become convicted while there and he needed someone to come get him. He didn't have a car. So R.W. went and picked him up. I have to give my ex credit; he would help anyone. He went and got the young man, who stayed at our house. That morning, I got up and fixed breakfast, and this was the beginning of the end of our so-called marriage.

The minister started being on the phone with him constantly. The young man would tell him, "You need to go spend time with your wife," and R.W. would say, "Oh, she's fine." From the young man's confession to me, the minister started asking him questions concerning his homosexual life and the lifestyle. The young man confessed to me all of this, and it was like opening up a can of worms that didn't need to be opened. He told me that R.W. was living promiscuously through his experiences. Although he could have chosen not to tell me, he did, and I really thank him for that. What I didn't tell you was that this young man was HIV-positive. He told both of us, because a lot of people didn't know. Well, their relationship got stronger, and R.W. didn't even want to sleep in the same bed as me. From that point, the abuse started again.

We were both in the ministry. I was an evangelist missionary, and he was an elder. Once I had an out of town engagement for which I was the main speaker, but I kept complaining that my side was hurting. So the minister just prayed for me, and the pain eased enough for me to preach. Then, when I got home, I was doubled over in pain. I told him that I needed to go to the hospital. Even though the hospital was near our house, I was in pain. He said, "Well, you better go to the hospital then." So I got in my car and drove myself to the hospital. Again, I was in shock. I couldn't understand why he would treat me like I was a dog. I ended up having to have surgery, but he really didn't care, because he really didn't love me. Ladies, if he even cared about my well-being, he would have at least helped me get to the hospital. He didn't love me.

1 Corinthians 13 tells us what love is. Let's see what it says. "Though I speak with the tongues of men and of angels, and have not charity [love] I am become as a sounding brass, or a tinkling cymbal. And though I have the gift of prophecy, and understand all mysteries, and all knowledge; and though I have all faith, so that I could remove mountains, and have not charity [love], I am nothing. And though I bestow all my goods to feed the poor, and though I give my body to be burned, and have not charity [love] it profiteth me nothing. Charity suffereth long, and is kind; charity envieth not; charity vaunteth not itself, is not puffed up, Doth not behave itself unseemly, seeketh not her own, is not easily provoked, thinketh no evil; Rejoiceth not in iniquity, but rejoiceth in the truth; Beareth all things, believeth all things, hopeth all things, endureth all things. Charity [love] never faileth: but whether there be prophecies, they

shall fail; whether there be tongues, they shall cease; whether there be knowledge, it shall vanish away. For we know in part, and we prophesy in part. But when that which is perfect is come, then that which is in part shall be done away. When I was a child, I spake as a child, I thought as a child: but when I became a man, I put away childish things. For now we see through a glass, darkly; but then face to face: now I know in part; but then shall I know even as also I am known. And now abideth, faith, hope, charity [love], these three; but the greatest of these is charity [love]." The Bible tells us what love is. What I was experiencing was not of God, and it wasn't a reflection of God's love for me. R.W. started throwing things at me again, like keys or whatever he had in his hand. He started pushing me up into the corners and hitting me.

I had surgery on a tooth that had broken off and needed to be extracted. It was bleeding really badly, and the dentist's office was near the young man's house that he had become close to. After the appointment, I went to his house; we were friends as well. I really needed to get some rest and get my strength back. I had asked God to let me find out the truth about what was really going on with him and my husband. I went over to his house, and the young man confessed to me, because it was bothering him, the things that were transpiring between him and my husband. He told me that my husband told him that he was in love with him, and that he had oral sex with him. I could see that this was hard for him to confess, but I thanked him for telling me the truth. I was hurt, but I didn't hold him totally responsible. He asked me to forgive him, because he never wanted me to be hurt. I truly believed that he was genuine. For someone to understand the lifestyle, he would have had to be bound by it and set free from it. I went home with my mouth being sore from the dentist,

The Battered Preacher's Wife

and I confronted my husband about what the young man had said. He said it was not true, but then he started fighting me. I began to call him names, and when he tried to push me down a flight of stairs, God protected me. Then I told him that I was divorcing him and it was over. I told him that I couldn't take anymore of this. I had given him six years of my life (well, a total of ten, because we dated for four), and I wasn't going to do it anymore. He said, "Well, I don't have any place to go." So I gave him thirty days to get out. That's when he got really crazy.

God sent one of the young ladies from the church to visit me; she told me that she had a dream of me stabbing my husband and killing him. She said that she saw me going to jail. Her dream was on point, because I was so angry with him. I had made up my mind that he wasn't going to hurt me or hit me anymore. I would go to bed with a screwdriver by my bed for protection. The house that I lived in was old, and I couldn't lock my bedroom door. I kept the dream in the back of my mind. The time for him to leave was counting down. He was trying everything to get me to stay with him, but my mind was made up. Well, one night I was in a very deep sleep. He came into my room while I was sleeping, and he raped me. He raped me like I was an animal. I woke up with his hands covering my mouth. He said, "When I had you, I didn't want you; now that I don't have you, I want you," and he raped me. I keep emphasizing that he raped me, because "you can be raped by your husband." I thought about stabbing him, but when I remembered the young lady's dream, I didn't do it. I stood still and allowed God to fight for me. He was so evil, because he didn't have to do that to me. He made the choice to do that. I cried for so long, and I washed so hard and for so long. I felt like I was a piece of dirt. Before he left, he tried to rape me again, but this time I was awake and alert. I saw the presence of an angel in the dining room. R.W. was grabbing me, and I pushed against him. Then he got behind me and tried to pull me from behind. Somehow it was like a force pushed him through the wall, and he stopped.

He eventually got his things and left, but he tried to get people from the church to tell me that I couldn't divorce him on the grounds of adultery. He had a counselor to come and try to say he was going in to this program to help people overcome homosexuality. I told them and him it was over. I prayed for his deliverance, but the marriage was over. I didn't look back. I went through so much once I finally said it was over. I had one pastor tell me that I didn't have the grounds to divorce him on the ground of adultery. He tried to get me to stay with him. I had stayed with R.W. for six years. I couldn't believe the pastor was trying to get me to stay. I said, "If a man did this to your daughter, would you tell her to stay?" The pastor's wife said, "No matter what you do, I will support you," and that's what I needed to hear. I had to take care of everything; all of the financial burdens were on me. He stuck me with so many bills, and he never paid his child support like he was supposed to.

It's not God's plan for us as women to be beaten and treated like we are some dirt on the ground. Women, no lady, girl, first lady, preacher's wife, or deacon's wife deserves to be treated like she is nothing. Ladies, you have to wake up. You have to stop covering for your husband; so many pastors' wives are being abused in some shape or form. Physical abuse is one form of abuse. Verbal abuse is just as bad. The abuser's goal is to take all your power and make you his slave. There's no difference between what you allow him to do to you and slavery. Whatever the master says, that's what you do. You are valuable, and if your husband is abusing you physically, sexually, verbally, or psychologically, then you need to recognize the value of your worth. You probably say, "I'm afraid; I don't have the strength." If you have the strength to stay, then you have the strength to leave. I know of the wives of so many pastors, preachers, ministers, and even deacons that are hiding, putting on makeup to cover the abuse that they are experiencing and wearing long sleeves to cover bruises. Some of you know that your husband is sleeping around with men and women, yet you say nothing and stay. But you are slowly dying. I don't think that there is anything in the wedding vows about him trying to kill you. It does say, "Till death do we part," but not, "Till you kill me."

People knew that my husband was controlling, overbearing, and always had to be the center of attention. They knew he was physically hurting me, but what could they do? It wasn't until I got sick and tired of being sick and tired that I left. You have to love yourself, and when you love yourself, you demand that people treat you with love and respect. Ladies, I know how it feels to be abused and feel like you are nothing. That's why I'm writing this book: to tell you that you can start your life over. God will restore the years that the enemy took away from you. Your best days are ahead. So many women get killed. You don't have to be the next one.

When I got the protection from abuse order, he still violated it. He came into the house when I wasn't there, moved things around, changed his dirty clothes, and left them in the floor just to let me know that he could do whatever he wanted. Well, I called the cops, and we went back to court. The judge told him that he would go to jail the next time he violated the order. He was scared of prison, and so he backed off. I filed for divorce at the end of 1998, and when he claimed he didn't get the papers, it delayed the process for another three months. Then in April of 1999, I divorced him.

I left the state and moved to the Maryland area. God gave me a new start. I had two beautiful daughters that I had to raise alone, and I did so with little to no child support. Currently, I receive no child support from him, and it's almost nine years later. He always got my addresses, and he used them to try to intimidate me. He would tell me stuff like, "I don't care where you go; I can always find you." I have many regrets, like the fact that all those times I left, I should have never gone back. But I do thank God for my beautiful daughters. He doesn't pay child support, and he has not been involved in my daughter's lives for almost nine years. I believed that once married, I could never get a divorce, because what I was taught in the church was that it doesn't matter what you go through at home with your husband. You are to keep your business at home, and if he beats you or cheats on you, then just stay there and thank God that you've got a man. This man could have given me a sexually transmitted disease, or worse, HIV or AIDS. I thank God that I didn't get it, but it could have happened. There are many cases where the abuser and cheater gave his innocent wife and unborn child AIDS or a sexually transmitted disease. You have to get out of any relationship that is killing you. This was killing me in every area of my life: physically, emotionally, and mentally. The church needs to rise up to help these women get out of these abusive and adulterous relationships, and it needs to stop telling them to keep their business at home. So many women have died or have been physically damaged for the rest of their lives because someone's pastor, minister, or evangelist told them to go back and let God work it out. There are so many pastor's wives, minister's wives, and deacon's wives that are victims of domestic violence. Listen to this true story of a friend of mine that was almost killed by her husband, who was a minister.

Chapter 7

My Friend's Story

Here is her story in her own words.

I was a battered minister's wife for approximately twelve years, because I was taught at the minister's wives meeting, "Keep your business at home, and cover your husband no matter what." That is exactly what I did. My former husband was abusive in many ways: sexually, emotionally, socially, financially, and physically. Throughout the entire time I was married to him, the children and I were in and out of shelters. When I was at the end of my third trimester, he struck me. I received an order of protection from the court, but with no money and no place to go, the judge told me to go home. There were times when my husband enforced a curfew on me, and I had to be in the house by 9:30 a.m. So if I was at a church function, either he would show up and tell me to come home, or I would return home to find the deadbolt lock on the door. Or the next day, when it was time for me to go to work, he would take the car keys so that I wouldn't have a way to work. Sometimes when people came to pick me up, they weren't allowed in the driveway. There were times I knew I would be late coming home, and so I started leaving a window open so that my daughter could climb through the window to open the door for me and my son.

He has had numerous affairs, and upon confronting him, he would say, "Yes, I did." He would say, "Since you can't do this position or you won't ____ my ____, I had to find someone else to do it." He was cruel. He told me many times, "Are you sure you aren't crazy?" He told me that no one loved me but him and that no one ever would, and for some strange reason, I believed him. I just believed in my heart, "He is a minister; when he preaches he preaches the truth. He knows the truth; I know he will get better." Our pastor knew about the police visits to our home; he knew about my husband's abusive and adulterous ways. Nonetheless, I was told to hang in there, pray, believe God, and it would get better. So if I left, I would always return, because I loved my husband. I didn't want to follow the footsteps of both of our parents (both of our fathers were abusive to their wives), and I wanted a father for our children.

After finding out about my husband's final affair, that was the end of the line for me. I came to my senses and said, "I am a queen, and I deserve to be treated like one. I am not his dirt; I am beautiful, educated, and intelligent." I filed for divorce. He pleaded and begged me not to go through with it, to go to counseling, etc. We had had counseling through the years, and every time we went, he quit. He even went to anger management class. So during the time we were separated, I would be driving down the road and would find him following me. One day while I was at work, a concerned parent called to tell me that he had had the lights and water at my house disconnected. I even woke up one morning and couldn't go to work because he had removed the car.

Even though we lived in our own separate places, one night in 2004 he broke down the door with a military dagger in his hand, yelling. He pierced me between the breasts, then pulled it out and tried to put the knife back in my chest. Because the children heard the ruckus, they came in to help, and our daughter suffered a wound as well. All of our children were thrown around the room like they were rag dolls. The next thing I knew, I was outside on the ground with the knife to my throat, and the only thing that came to my mind to say was, "What about all that praying and fasting and laying before the Lord you were just doing?" Then he dropped me and walked off. As the children and I started to try to make it over to my neighbor's home, I saw car lights. I thought it was the police, but it was him trying to run us over with his car. Then he jumped out and tried to stab me with a screwdriver, but my neighbors stopped him. I sustained injury to my heart, lungs, hands, and back. I was hospitalized in ICU for a week. The kids and I were homeless for six months, and I was unable to work and care for them and myself. About a month after the stabbing, I was still unable to walk far distances, because it was hard for me to breathe. I contracted pneumonia and had muscle problems with my legs. I asked for financial and emotional support from my pastor and church congregation, and I received nothing, not even a $1.00 card.

We have continued to suffer with fear of his continued harassing letters and calls, even though he was instructed not to do that. Just recently, he pleaded guilty to the crime, but due to his claiming that his one year tour of duty as a reservist made him crazy, he received one year in prison and three years of probation. The children and I continue to suffer on a daily basis, mostly emotionally and financially, while he gets a check for claiming he is crazy. I continue to trust my Father above and Him only.

This story is true, and I tried to counsel this young lady to leave when he threatened to kill her and get away with it. It's sad but true that the church supported him, but no one went to check on the true victims. No one went to check on the woman or the kids that lived through this horrific attack. The church sent a representative to the prison to encourage him when he served six months. What is six months? This man stabbed his wife in front of his children, tried to run them over with his car, then tried to stab her again with a screwdriver, and he did this all in front of his children. It just doesn't seem fair. This woman is one of many, one of many. She just lived to tell her story. Others didn't make it. When are the men and women of God going to stand up and say that enough is enough? Well, I am standing up to say that the church can't keep telling women to go home and keep silence about their abusive husbands, no matter if it's the pastor, preacher, or deacon. Women internalize all the abuse and blame themselves for it.

Woman of God, it's not your fault; you don't deserve to be treated like dirt. You are royalty; rise up and get out of the marriage. Do it for your children. We are telling our children that it is okay to let a man abuse you. If a man wants to change, he can. You must put yourself first.

Chapter 8

Domestic Violence and the Black Church Statistics

It is estimated that every 9 seconds, a woman is battered- The Department of Justice, 1991

Domestic Violence is any coercive behavior that is used by one adult over another in an intimate relationship. It consists of any type of abuse, which may be one or a combination of any of the following types:

 -*physical (beating)*
 -*verbal (threats)*
 -*sexual (rape)*
 -*economic (taking her money)*
 -*psychological (mind games)*

Domestic Violence is often overlooked as "a lovers' quarrel" or a "private family matter," but it is an epidemic that affects women of every class, race, sexual orientation and religion.

Ninety to ninety-five percent of domestic violence victims are women, and many of these women are active members in their local churches.

General Statistics About Domestic Violence
- ❖ *Nearly 2 in 3 female victims of violence were related to or knew their attacker. Over two-thirds of violent victimizations against women were committed by someone known to them: 31% of female victims reported that the offender was a stranger. Approximately 28% were intimates such as husbands or boyfriends, 35% were acquaintances, and the remaining 5% were other relatives.*
- ❖ *In a New York study of 50 battered women, 75% said they had been harassed by the batterer while they were at work, 50% reported missing an average of three days per month, and 44% lost at least one job for reasons directly related to the abuse.*
- ❖ *In a national survey of over 6,000 American families, 50% of the men who frequently assaulted their wives also frequently abused their children.*
- ❖ *One-third of all female homicide victims are killed by husbands, ex-husbands, boyfriends or ex-boyfriends.*
- ❖ *In a study of females killed by intimate partners between 1980-1982, it was found that the majority of women killed were married (57.7%, n=2,415). Girlfriends were the next highest percentage (24.5% n-1,041).*
- ❖ *The March of Dimes reports that pregnant women are at particular risk of being battered by spouses. More babies are now being born with birth defects as a result of the*

mother being battered during pregnancy than from the combination of all the diseases for which we immunize pregnant women.

- *Wife-beating results in more injuries that require medical treatment than rape, auto accidents, and muggings combined.*
- *In the United States, a woman is more likely to be assaulted, injured, raped, or killed by a male partner than any other assailant.*

A poem from a Battered Woman
(Author Unknown)

I WAS HUNGRY

I was abused by my partner, and you told me to stay because it was the Lord's will.

I became hungry because I could not work, and you formed a humanities club and discussed hunger. Thank you.

My clothes became worn and torn, exposing my naked body, and in your mind, you debated the morality of my appearance.

At times I became seriously ill because of my lack of nutrients, and you knelt and thanked God for your health.

I was thrown out of my house, and you preached to me of the spiritual shelter of the love of God.

I was abandoned and became lonely, and you left me alone to pray for me.

You seem so holy, so close to God. But I'm still being abused. I'm still hungry, lonely, and cold.

When I Call for Help: a Pastoral Response to Domestic Violence Against Women.

In the beginning, I was young, and he was handsome. He said that I was beautiful, smart, and worthy of love, and he made me feel that way. So we were married, walking joyfully together down a church aisle, our union blessed by God.

Then come the angry words, the verbal tearing apart. Now I am made to feel ugly, unintelligent, and unworthy of any love, God's or man's. Next come the beatings: unrelenting violence and unceasing pain. I shouldn't stay, but this is my husband, to whom I am promised forever. He says I deserve it; maybe I do. If I could just be good, maybe he would stop. I feel so alone. Doesn't God hear me when I cry out silently as I lie in bed each night?

Finally came the release, the realization. It was not me; it was him. I was worthy of love, God's and man's. One spring morning, my heart was filled with hope and with only the fear of starting over on my own. And so again I walked down the hallway of our apartment building, never again to be silent, never again to live with that kind of violence or to suffer that kind of pain.

This response was written by a battered wife
(Author Unknown)

Chapter 9

The Catholic Church View

As pastors of the Catholic Church in the United States, we state as clearly and strongly as we can that violence against women, inside or outside the home, is never justified. Violence in any form-"physical, sexual, psychological, or verbal"-is sinful; often, it is a crime as well. We have called for a moral revolution to replace a culture of violence. We acknowledge that violence has many forms, many causes, and many victims-men as well as women.

The Catholic Church teaches that violence against another person in any form fails to treat that person as someone worthy of love. Instead, it treats the person as an object to be used. When violence occurs within a sacramental marriage, the abused spouse may question, "How do these violent acts relate to my promise to take my spouse for better or for worse? " The person being assaulted needs to know that acting to end the abuse does not violate the marriage promises. While violence can be directed towards men, it tends to harm women and children more.

In 1992 we spoke out against domestic violence. We called on the Christian community to work vigorously against it. Since then, many dioceses, parishes, and organizations have made domestic violence a priority issue. We commend and encourage these efforts.

In this update of our 1992 statement, we again express our desire to offer the Church's resources to both the women who are abused and the men who abuse. Both groups need Jesus' strength and healing. We focus here on violence against women, since 85 percent of the victims of reported cases of non-lethal domestic violence are women. Women's greatest risk of violence comes from intimate partners-a current former husband or boyfriend.

Violence against women in the home has serious repercussions for children. Over 50 percent of men who abuse their wives also beat their children. Children who grow up in violent homes are more likely to develop alcohol and drug addictions and to become abusers themselves. The stage is set for a cycle of violence that may continue from generation to generation.

The Church can help break this cycle. Many abused women seek help first from the Church because they see it as a safe place. Even if their abusers isolate them from other social contacts, they may still allow them to go to church. Recognizing the critical role that the Church can play, we address this statement to several audiences:

- To women who are victims of violence and who many need the Church's help to break out of their pain and isolation;
- To pastors, parish personnel, and educators, who are often the first responders for abused women;
- To men who abuse and may not know how to break out of the cycle of violence; and
- To society, which has made some strides towards recognizing the extent of domestic violence against women.

We recognize that violence against women has many dimensions. This statement is not meant to be all-inclusive, but rather to be an introduction, along with some practical suggestions of what dioceses and parishes can do now.

An Overview of Domestic Violence

Domestic violence is any kind of behavior that a person uses to control an intimate partner through fear and intimidation. It includes physical, sexual, psychological, verbal and economic abuse. Some examples of domestic abuse include battering, name-calling and insults, threats to kill or harm one's partner or children, destruction of property, marital rape, and forced sterilization or abortion.

Younger, unmarried women are at greatest risk for domestic violence. According to a U.S. government survey, 53 percent of victims were abused by a current or former girlfriend or boyfriend. One-third of all victims were abused by a spouse while 14 percent said that the offender was an ex-spouse. Women ages 16 to 24 are nearly three times as vulnerable to attacks by imitate partners as those in other age groups; abuse victims between ages 35 and 49 run the highest risk and being killed.

While abuse cuts across all ethnic and economic backgrounds, some women face particular obstacles. Women of color may not view the criminal justice system as a source of help. Additionally, in some cultures women feel pressured to keep problems within the home and to keep the family together at all costs. Some fear that they will lose face in the community if they leave. Immigrant women often lack familiarity with the language and legal systems of this country. Their abusers may threaten them with deportation.

Women in rural communities may find themselves with fewer resources. The isolation imposed by distance and lack of transportation can aggravate their situation. Isolation can also be a factor for women who do not work outside the home. They may have less access to financial resources and to information about domestic violence. Women with disabilities and elderly women are also particularly vulnerable to violence.

Some who suffer from domestic violence are also victims of stalking, which includes following a person, making harassing phone calls, and vandalizing property. Eight percent of women in the United States have been stalked at some time in their lives, and more than one million are stalked annually. Stalking is a unique crime because stalkers are obsessed with controlling their victims' actions and feelings. A victim can experience extreme stress, rage, depression, and an inability to trust anyone.

Domestic violence is often shrouded in silence. People outside the family hesitate to interfere, even when they suspect abuse is occurring. Many times even extended family denies that abuse exists, out of loyalty to the abuser and in order to protect the image of the family. Some people still argue-mistakenly-that intervention by outside sources endangers the sanctity of the home. Yet abuse and assault are no less serious when they occur within a family. Even when domestic violence is reported, sometimes there are failures to protect victims adequately or to punish perpetrators.

Why Men Batter

Domestic violence is learned behavior. Men who batter learn to abuse through observation, experience, and reinforcement. They believe that they have a right to use violence; they are also rewarded, that is, their behavior gives them power and control over their partner.

Abusive men come from all economic classes, races, religions, and occupations. The batterer may be a "good provider" and a respected member of his church and community. While there is no one type, men who abuse share some common characteristics. They tend to be extremely jealous, possessive, and easily angered. A man may fly into a rage because his spouse called her mother too often or because she didn't take the car in for servicing. Many try to isolate their partners by limiting their contact with family and friends.

Typically, abusive men deny that the abuse is happening, or they minimize it. They often blame their abusive behavior on someone or something other than themselves. They tell their partner, "You made me do this"

Many abusive men hold a view of women as inferior. Their conversation and language reveal their attitude towards a woman's place in society. Many believe that men are meant to dominate and control women.

Alcohol and drugs are often associated with domestic violence, but they do not cause it. An abusive man who drinks or uses drugs has two distinct problems: substance abuse and violence. Both must be treated.

Why Women Stay

Women stay with men who abuse them primarily out of fear. Some fear that they will lose their children. Many believe that they cannot support themselves, much less their children.

When the first violent act occurs, the woman is likely to be incredulous. She believes her abuser when he apologizes and promises that it will not happen again. When it does-repeatedly-many women believe that if they just act differently they can stop the abuse. They may be ashamed to admit that the man they love is terrorizing them. Some cannot admit or realize that they are battered women. Others have endured trauma and suffer from battered woman syndrome.

REMEMBER: Some battered women run a high risk of being killed when they leave their abuser or seek help from the legal system. It is important to be honest with women about the risks involved. If a woman decides to leave, she needs to have a safety plan, including the names and phone numbers of shelters and programs. Some victims may choose to stay at this time because it seems safer. Ultimately, abused women must make their own decisions about staying or leaving..

The Church Responds to Domestic Violence
Scripture and Church Teachings

Religion can be either a resource or a roadblock for battered women. As a resource, it encourages women to resist mistreatment. As a roadblock, its misinterpretation can contribute to the victim's self-blame and suffering and to the abuser's rationalizations.

Abused women often say, "I can't leave this relationship. The Bible says it would be wrong," Abusive men often say, "The Bible says my wife should be submissive to me. "They take the biblical text and distort it to support their right to batter. As bishops, we condemn the use of the Bible to support abusive behavior in any form. A correct reading of Scripture leads people to understanding of the equal dignity of men and women and to relationships based on mutuality and love. Beginning with Genesis, Scripture teaches that women and men are created in God's image. Jesus himself always respected the human dignity of women. Pope John Paul II reminds us "Christ's way of acting, the Gospel of his words and deeds, is a consistent protest against whatever offends the dignity of women.

Men who abuse often use Ephesians 5:22, taken out of context, to justify their behavior, but the passage (v. 21-33) refers to the mutual submission of husband and wife out of love for Christ. Husbands should love their wives as they love their own body, as Christ loves the Church.

Men who batter also cite Scripture to insist that their victims forgive them (see, for example, Mt 6: 9-15) a victim then feels guilty if she cannot do so. Forgiveness, however, does not mean forgetting the abuse or pretending that it did not happen. Neither is possible. Forgiveness is not permission to repeat the abuse. Rather, forgiveness means that the victim decides to let go of the experience and move on with greater insight and conviction not to tolerate abuse of any kind again.

An abused woman may see her suffering as just punishment for a past deed for which she feels guilty. She may try to explain suffering by saying that it is God's Will or "part of God's plan for my life "or" God's way of teaching me a lesson." This image of a harsh, cruel God runs contrary to the biblical image of a kind, merciful, and loving God. Jesus went out of his way to help suffering women. Think of the woman with the hemorrhage (Mk. 5:25-34) or the woman caught in adultery (John 8:1-11) God promises to be present to us in our suffering, even when it is unjust. Finally we emphasize that no person is expected to stay in an abusive marriage. Some abused women believe that church teaching on the permanence of marriage requires them to stay in an abusive relationship. They may hesitate to seek a separation or divorce. They may fear that they cannot re-marry in the Church. Violence and abuse, not divorce, break up a marriage. We encourage abused persons who have divorced to investigate the possibility of seeking an annulment. An annulment, which determines that the marriage bond is not valid, can frequently open the door to healing.

First Responders: Priests, Deacons, and Lay Ministers

Many Church ministers want to help abused women but worry that they are not experts on domestic violence. Clergy may hesitate to preach about domestic violence because they are unsure what to do if an abused woman approaches them for help.

We ask them to keep in mind that intervention by church ministers has three goals, in the following order:

1. Safety for the victim and children
2. Accountability for the abuser; and
3. Restoration of the relationship (if possible), or mourning over the loss of the relationship.

We also encourage church ministers to see themselves as "first responders" who
Listen to and believe the victim's story
Help her to assess the danger to herself and her children,
Refer her to counseling and other specialized services.

Church ministers should become familiar with and follow the reporting requirements of their state. Many professionals who deal with vulnerable people are required to report suspected crimes, which may include domestic abuse. In dealing with people who abuse, church ministers need to hold them accountable for their behavior. They can support the abusive person as he seeks specialized counseling to change his abusive behavior. Couple counseling is not appropriate and can endanger the victim's safety.

What You Can Do to Help
For Abused Women

Begin to believe that you are not alone and that help is available for you and your children. Talk in confidence to someone you trust: a relative, friend, parish priest, deacon, religious sister or brother, or lay minister. If you choose to stay in the situation, at least for now, set up a plan of action to ensure your safety. This includes hiding a car key, personal documents, and some money in a safe place and locating somewhere to go in an emergency.

Find out about resources in your area that offer help to battered women and their children. The phone book lists numbers to call in your local area.

For Men Who Abuse

Admit that abuse is your problem, not your partner's, and have the manly courage to seek help. Begin to believe that you can change your behavior if you choose to do so.

Be willing to reach out for help. Talk to someone you trust who can help you evaluate the situation.

Keep in mind that the Church is available to help you. Part of the mission Jesus entrusted to us is to offer healing when it is needed.

Find alternative ways to act when you become frustrated or angry. Talk to other men who have overcome abusive behavior. Find out what they did and how they did it.

For Pastors and Pastoral Staff

Make sure your parish is a safe place where abused women and abusive men can come for help. Here are some specific suggestions:

Include information about domestic violence and local resources in parish bulletins and newsletters and on websites.

Place copies of this brochure and/or other information, including local telephone numbers for assistance about domestic violence, in women's restroom (s).

Keep an updated list of resources for abused women. This can project for the parish pastoral council, social justice committee, or women's group.

Find a staff person or volunteer who is willing to receive in-depth training on domestic violence; ask this person to serve as a resource and to help educate others about abuse.

Provide training on domestic violence to all church ministers, including priests, deacons and lay ministers. When possible, provide opportunities for them to hear directly from victims of violence.

Join in the national observance of October as Domestic Violence Awareness Month. Dedicate at least one weekend that month to inform parishioners about domestic abuse. During that month, make available educational and training programs in order to sensitize men and women, girls and boys to the personal and social effects of violence in the family. Help them to see how psychological abuse may escalate over time.

Teach them how to communicate without violence.

Chapter 10

Conclusion

I am not condemning anyone who is a homosexual. I am just telling my story; so please don't get mad at me. This is the land of the free, the home of the brave. We all have a right of freedom of speech, just as I have a right to freedom of speech. Jesus died for the sins of the world, and no one is struggling with anything that God can't help him overcome. I often ask myself, *why*, but you have to turn that *why* into a *thank God that I'm still alive*. I know of a situation (I will not mention names) of a lady whose husband died. She married a deacon in the church, and he started physically abusing her. So she left and went to her pastor, who told her that God was going to work it out and to go back to her husband. She did, and he brutally murdered her. You don't want to allow that to happen to you. I know that some of you are saying, "That will not happen to me." I thought that way, too, until I saw that rage in his eyes. And in that moment, I knew he could have easily killed me. If they can hit you, they can easily kill you. One hit can be fatal. So many women have listened to others telling them, "Hold on, and he will change." Change has to come from within. I am still suffering today. My neck, back, wrist, and my ear are all damaged. I live in pain, and I learned to deal with it. It's a risk to leave, but you take a risk staying. Let my life be an example to you. God loves you, and it is not His will for anyone to abuse you.

My ex-husband, after he fought me, then wanted to be intimate; it's the classic cycle of the abuser to cry, to apologize, to say that he really is sorry, and then to try to use sex as a means to make up. In my mind, it's perverted. You are bruised up and crying, and he is trying to be intimate. It's sick. I don't care who you are or how large your church is. If your husband is being unfaithful to you and physically abusing you, then you need to do something: leave. I know I was ashamed. I was married to a known preacher and prophet, who was known for praying for people and prophesying them into their destinies, but he never dealt with his own issues. I have to say that God did use him to help many people spiritually, but he wouldn't allow the God that he preached about to help him overcome his demons.

I don't deal with this young man. He continues to send letters, but he doesn't financially support my children. My current husband took them as his own, and he has provided them with everything that they need. God made up to me in a big way. Yes, although my new husband and I have gone through many trials and tribulations, he loves me, and he's a good man. He has never physically or emotionally abused me. He takes care of five children and me, and all of our needs are met. There are a lot of good men that are raising someone else's children. Men, you keep up the good work: God is going to bless you. I like to use the phrase that just because you donate sperm, that does not a father make. The Bible says that if you don't take care of your own, you are less than an infidel. (I

Timothy 5:8) Thank you, honey, for being my gift from God. We have come through a lot, but you continue to strive to be a better man and father. Although he had family members telling him not to marry me, he chose to believe God, and we are blessed because of it. I love you with all of me. Ladies, women, and young ladies, God will give you a man that loves you, respects you, and treats you the way God ordained for a man to treat his wife.

Don't believe the lie that no one will ever want you. That's not true. I left, moved to another state, and started my life over. I had some pastors telling me that I didn't have grounds to divorce the minister, but when I heard an audible voice say, "You are free," and when I had done everything that I could do, I got out of there. It shouldn't have taken six years. I should have left sooner, but I left. Please get out. Don't stay. Do it for your children if you can't do it for yourself. Let me leave you with this Scripture passage that I quoted earlier about what love is from 1 Corinthians. Love never puts down, demeans or tries to kill. God doesn't require that we stay in an abusive marriage. God's thoughts toward you are good and not evil to give you an expected end. Jeremiah 29:11 (KJV)

The resources that are shared give pastors and leader tools to use, because domestic violence is happening in the pulpit. We can close our eyes, or we can get involved and let all involved know that they can be healed and restored if they take the steps to change and commit to work hard to turn their life around. In conclusion, God is a God of restoration, but in my case the abuser did not really want to change. To change, the abuser has to have a realization that he is an abuser, and he has to work hard to stop the cycle of abuse. If he doesn't work hard, then he will continue to go around in circles. That's what happened in my situation. You can go to counseling, but if you don't do what the counselor says, then you have chosen to follow your own path. That's the path of abuse.

I know what it feels like to be abused. I know what it feels like to want to be loved. I know what it feels like to want to be valued. I know what it feels like to want to be respected. I know what it feels like to go through the healing process. That's a big healing process, one that many men and women want to avoid. I could not have endured all the things I endured and now be able to talk about it and be transparent concerning my life, if I didn't go through the healing process. God took all of my pain, anger, and bitterness away. Well, why did He take it? He took it because I asked Him to, and I was willing to let go of all the pain. I could not help others receive healing and deliverance if I myself had never experienced the healing power of God. I survived, and you are a survivor. You deserve to be loved and respected, not abused, disheveled, and rejected. God loves you more than anyone else can. You must first love yourself and value yourself, and then you will have the power to get out of that abusive relationship. Be blessed.

If you haven't asked the Lord Jesus into your life, or if you strayed away from Him, then just repeat this prayer with me. *I believe that Jesus Christ is the Son of God and that He died on the cross just for me. I ask You, God, to forgive me for all of my sins, come into my heart, come into my life, save me, and make me clean.* You are a new creation. Read Romans 10:9 (KJV). Says That if thou shalt confess with thy mouth the Lord Jesus, and believe in thine heart that God hath raised him from the dead, thou shalt be saved.

Chapter 11

General Information

There are certain signs that categorize someone as an abuser. This is a list of things to look for in an abuser or if someone is a showing sign of becoming a potential abuser.

- Abuser may appear to be a normal individual.
- Abuser may show remorse for things done or said.
- Abuser may even get emotional and cry.
- Abuser will sometimes have alternate personalities.
- Abuser displays acts of control and dominance.
- Abuser will often express shame, fear, and the need to do himself / herself bodily harm.
- Abuser may not use the same form of abuse with each incident.
- Abuser is crafty and persuasive.
- Abuser will not admit guilt, but will direct it towards the victim.
- Abuser always promises to change for the better.

- Abuser believes that the victim made him / her do it. He / she was pushed into the violent act.
- Abuser isolates you from your friends and family.
- Abuser blames others for his problems.
- Abuser criticizes or insults you in public or in private.
- Abuser has unrealistic expectations of you in public or in private.
- Abuser ignores your feelings.
- Abuser is possessive, jealous, or harasses you about imagined relationships.
- Abuser threatens to hurt you, your children, family, or friends.
- Abuser manipulates you with lies and contradictions.

If you are in an abusive relationship, you need to make an intelligent decision to get out of it. You must overcome fear. If you stay, you are taking a risk. If you leave, you are taking a risk, but at least you have the courage to stand up for yourself and to take yourself and your power back.

Organizations that can give you assistance in Maryland:

- National Domestic Violence Hotline (800) 799-SAFE (7233)
- National Child Protective Services (800) 4-A-Child
- Victim Witness Assistance Program (consult your local listings)
- National Sexual Assault Hotline (800) 656-HOPE3

Websites That Can provide Assistance for Victims:

- Center for the Prevention of Sexual and Domestic Violence www.cpsdv.org

- National Domestic Violence Hotline: www.ndvh.org
- National Coalition Against Domestic Violence www.ncadv.org
- Family Violence Prevention Fund: www.endabuse.org

www.ingramcontent.com/pod-product-compliance
Ingram Content Group UK Ltd.
Pitfield, Milton Keynes, MK11 3LW, UK
UKHW041954230426
12048UKWH00008B/336